CW01086433

Always This Falling

poems by CAROLYN LOCKE

Produced by Maine Authors Publishing, Rockland, Maine
www.MaineAuthorsPublishing.com

Printed in the United States of America

*For my mother, Eva R. Russell, whose songs were the beginning,
and my father, Raymond T. Russell, whose optimism endures*

ACKNOWLEDGMENTS

I would like to thank the editors of the following publications in which versions of these poems first appeared:

Anthology of the Live Poets Society: "March Thaw" and "Regeneration"

Maine in Print: "Say It Was Autumn" and "At the Center"

Off the Coast: "A Gesture," "Blossom," and "Always This Falling"

Puckerbrush Review: "Margie Edwards Fogg"

Switched-on-Gutenberg: "A Reckoning"

The Waldo Independent: "French Bread"

"Always This Falling" was reprinted in the November 2009 issue of *Bangor Metro*, Tori Britton, Founding Editor, and Melanie Brooks, Managing Editor.

Heartfelt thanks: to Kathleen Ellis, Jaime Manrique, Michael Klein, Joan Larkin, and Nora Mitchell, who encouraged and inspired me early in the process of writing; to Chrystal Wing, Lucinda Garthwaite, Jim Reed, Jim Clark, Mark Wallace, and Helen Tirone, who read and critiqued this version of the manuscript; to Linda Lord, Sheila Gilluly, and Tanya Hubbard for their friendship and unfailing support and enthusiasm; to the many participants in the Clockworks Writers Conference and our WIPPOD group, as well as my Waldo County writing group, for suggestions on some of these poems; and to my husband, Gerry, and children, Jeff and Alison, for their love and encouragement.

CONTENTS

BALANCING

These days, I am wanting to follow the roots of maples
into their dark, thick places. Ride them
as they muscle their way into solid earth.
What is required to shrink yourself
into the smallest space
in which existence
is possible?
What is required to learn
if this hard-packed soil is as open as the universe, if
the distances between grains are,
as the poets claim, as great as light-years
between stars?

What am I to tell the self
who warns, *Stop sinking into that hole?*

What do I know? Only that even from here
the sky is visible—pale pink bleeds
into paler blue—and the shadows of the geranium
are sharp against the white wall.
Only that I can still hear
the call of the phoebe that used to stir
my morning blood.

Only that I am pulled downward
like a spiraling funnel,
digging deeper and deeper,
as earth closes her wide mouth,
and all that is left
is to drill silently
toward one still point.

MARCH THAW

Anyone who's traveled this road
knows what to expect
on the long stretch from solstice
to equinox.

How the surface buckles
and heaves when light begins
to unlock the earth. How pavement
crumbles to black dust,

leaving potholes deep enough
to lose you. How shadows
cover those unexpected dips
until you're in them. Anyone

who's been here knows,
when thaw rattles muscle and bone,
how silent red buds claw
at the closed chambers of the heart.

DISCLOSURES

These glasses, these plates, they talk
among themselves . . . Interminable disclosures.
-Paul Cézanne

She can't stop staring
at the butter-yellow tulips
framed in the bottom window
of the door—it's something
about a perfect rectangle,
the way the globed flowers lift
away from their stiff stems
toward the wooden sash
and never reach it—

something about the deep
grass behind them, broken
by the curve of soil—
that lets her breathe the cups
of their bodies
into her own, petals
swimming through her lungs, uncurling
against the walls of her veins.

And she can't stop looking
at the house on the corner,
how each time she gets to the end
of the road, the white clapboards
startle her into feeling the frame
of blue sea, emerald lawn,
hot-pink weigela—asymmetrical weights
pulling against the anchor
of the granite ledge.

FROM ACADIA MOUNTAIN

We're at the summit.
Below us, a small body in red climbs the foremast,
dives out over the edge. The moment
is the perfect arc of his body
just before it merges
with water.

Here in my garden
the blue-green hummingbird darts through the rain,
hovers at the tip of crimson, his body
an electric joining
of earth and sky.

Are all bodies
only this: muscle joining one thing to another
in the moment when we lose ourselves
to what we love?

My head leans
toward the hand that holds
this pen, muscles contract and expand,
trace each thought
as it leaps
to the next,

like that man
blowing the sax, his fingers
becoming brass keys, his love curving
through the arc
of the horn.

A GESTURE

Even the cats are starving in Morocco:
bony bodies, raw sores behind their ears,
on their backs and legs. Almost invisible

they lie on the cobbled paths or dusty streets,
walk gingerly on terrace walls, and quickly
disappear. The streets of the medina are rich

with the smells of oranges, apples, lemons,
strawberries, and melons, pungent with paprika,
saffron, and mustard, with the earthy scent

of carrots and potatoes, sweet lettuce—
and everywhere the sharpness of mint.
Here, where abundance is overwhelming,

the swell of bodies glides in elegant djellabas
of turquoise, orange, maroon, lime green,
and in the shadowed corners, random bodies

huddle camouflaged in gray or tan,
heads resting against stucco walls,
hands on their laps, palms up.

Sometimes a mouth moves without sound,
one thin hand reaches out,
catches your eye, and you see

the tendons and bones of an arm
exposed as the sleeve of a robe slides down,
eyes moving beneath closed lids.

You quickly turn away, then back again,
hear the echo of your returning footsteps
on stone, want your hesitation

to be read as a good omen,
to give a bit of hope. The eyes
never open, but still you reach down

and place a coin in the open palm.
The arrogance of your action
prickles down your spine.

POINT OF ENTRY

Ever since the sun dropped below the horizon,
I've been nudging the corners of darkness.
Up ahead, blue lights flash in the subzero night,
directing me down the Crocker Road, a detour
that winds through the frozen landscape,
my only beacon the glow of red taillights
in the distance. I am uneasy

depending on the knowledge of others.
We turn left and left and left again,
a bright half-moon hanging in the winter sky
while the tinny sound of steel drums
fills the car with the heat of Caribbean sun.
Up ahead lights flash again—
red and blue fingering the black night

like strobes pulsing in a dark room.
No detours this time. I approach with caution.
Forced to stop and wait, unable to resist,
I peer into the darkness. On the roadside,
silhouettes glowing like coals in a dying fire
huddle around a nest of cars. Off to the right,
the gray outline of a telephone pole

hangs like a crucifix from the wires,
and just beyond, crushed metal penetrates deep
into the brush. There is no sign of life.
My foot touches the gas pedal,
inches the car forward into the world
on the other side, all houses now in darkness
except for the occasional flicker
of candlelight from deep inside. I imagine
the moment of impact—metal against wood,
the body's continuing momentum propelling it
against the steering wheel, the soul
fleeing its comfortable cave of flesh,
spiraling into the vast emptiness,
its sharp light a white wound in the wheeling sky.

WOMEN RISING

for Tanya

1

You tell me you are a freak, a woman
who will lose her hair,
the cancer like original sin
banishing you from the garden.

2

you said i could call you
any time i needed
even at 3 a.m.
then laughed at yourself
said it was a foolish thought
that i might wake
with thoughts of you
and so i couldn't tell you then
how i had spent the long night
listening to the howling winds watching
the revolving light of the sand truck
bob along the walls a flickering
yellow presence that pulsed
like the words in my brain couldn't
tell you about the sparse moments
of dreaming when my throat
was a trumpet without breath
the only reverberation a dull ache
in my heart your words circling
around and around until i thought
i would go mad couldn't tell you
how the luminous red numbers
on the clock stood still how hours
passed between 3:05 and 3:10 how
i was falling off the edge of the earth
with you how time was not time was
only the gaping hole of my mind
me a pebble bouncing against
jagged walls couldn't tell you
how the wound in my breast
awakened as if it had heard
you crying

3
Can you see the women rising
like ghosts out of their own bodies
searching for some lost part
of themselves? how they
stand on the banks of the river
bearing bread they have kneaded
with firm hands, soup
they have simmered for hours,
scented soaps for the bath,
daisies, iris, carnations—
as if like the sirens they might waken
your senses, lure you back
across the river that cuts
the land between us? Words
are stopped in our mouths
but the gifts,
the gifts in our hands, are calling.

ROOTING AROUND

for Alison

chipped cobalt cup, rusted rake with a missing tooth,
arm chair oozing stuffing from its seat and back, a red-
spiked heel tossed into the junkyard of my mind with
coils of bedsprings, a dented car bumper, faded melmac
plate, tintype wedding portrait, pages of a girlie magazine
flipping in the breeze, leg of a mahogany table—

and now this morning there's what you left behind when
you weren't looking: a glass of rust-colored water for
washing brushes, cut up magazines strewn across your
bedroom floor, piles of limp shorts, socks turned inside
out, candle wax stuck to the surface of desk and dresser—

later, someone, or something, goes rooting around, piecing
together a crazy collage so vivid I can see it glimmer in
some distant landscape even at high noon when i'm busy
trying to weed a neat garden bordered by even stones, when
i'm working so hard to ignore the red satin pump, the limp
shorts, half-hidden in the leafy phlox, whispering, *listen to me*—

listen.

THE LACE MAKER

after Vermeer

Caught somewhere in the space
between her hands and eyes,
I bend with the lace maker
over her stitching,
fall into the lemon light,
drink the cream and royal blue of the cloth,
finger the scarlet flashes
that break the quiet moment.

I imagine her delicate weavings—
how they will graze the blue web of veins
that pulse in the wrists
of solid country women,
how flickering lamplight
will make shadows ripple
over hands that cup
the newborn's skull. Then wonder
if instead this lace will bear the weight
of steaming cups, bowls laden
with stew, plates of coarse bread,
thick goblets of red wine. And I think,

maybe all we need in this world
is fine cotton thread for weaving.

BLOSSOM

In the hour just before dawn
she is afraid
of being a boneless flower—

frightened by the softness
of petal skin,
the ease with which it is torn.

She wants the fist of morning
to grip
the tight bud of her body.

Maybe sometime, a shimmer of thread
will spin out of her center
and she will unfold,

tiptoe along its slippery length
into the open palm of afternoon.
And maybe sometime, she will even

let her petals fall, see
if there are any bones
to strut beneath the moon.

THE HEALING STONE

Hold this slice of stone
between fingers. Stroke
the circular paths of its layers—
light and dark, light and dark,
then lighter still.

Drift among its carved arches.
Let yourself be pulled
into the pulsing center.

Feel how the white arc
of your thumb
sparks fiery bands of heat.
Let them sear
the telltale prints
of your fingers.

Now, on this cliff,
dizzy with sunlight,
follow the arc of waves
that circle the granite shore.

See how they swirl and mesmerize,
how what goes out
mingles with what comes in,
how they breathe together.

Breathe.

AT THE KEEPER'S HOUSE

For days, black clouds hunch
in the western sky
and we skirt the edge
of storms. Distant thunder
stirs dark memories
behind us,
making us want
to turn back.

But we move forward,
board the boat to this island,
this house, this room
of white walls, tables, and chairs,
window frames that echo
the gray-green quiet
of the sea.

Here we are learning
to breathe again,
to let the wavering orange sun
pull us from our chairs,
from the room,
from the house.

We follow it, hands joined,
and float on calm waters,
letting waves ripple
over our faces and collect
in the hollows of our throats.

REGENERATION

for Gerry

I heard how the starfish learns the world
through touch, how its chemical sense
leads it to the mussel bed, how it feels
its way around crevices sucking soft bodies
from their shells. You can't kill a starfish
in any usual way—chop one up
and it multiplies, filling the waters
with quintuples of spiny legs
reaching out from humped backs, and curling
around the deep purple shells on the rocky
bottom. Sometimes I think I know
what it is to know the world
through only the body. If I close my eyes,
I no longer feel where my body ends
and yours begins—
and I can believe your hands are mine
reaching for muscle,
a strange body becoming my own,
and in my ear an unfamiliar heartbeat
pumps new blood, breath no longer mine
doubles the lungs, my need
growing larger than what any body can hold
until there is only this way of knowing, this touch
that leads me, blind as the starfish,
to become what I cannot see.

NIGHT OF THE NEW MOON

Just today, the white mushroom
must have sprung from the earth,
edges of its cap curling skyward
until it was a bowl for holding stars.

All this, while we sat in cultured silence
and the clock chimed eight, inviting the poet
to speak of women in blue silk, naked men
pressing their bodies against them.

Still, in the ebony night, the mushroom
grew its own flesh, petals of ivory phlox
caught the sheen of the starlit sky,
and our need grew large, and larger,

our restless bodies cupping themselves
around it until, the poet finally silent,
we walked out and called in the garden
to bring it back, the white cat
we had sent to hunt the darkness.

THE HAWSER

This is how it looked: golden
in a thin translucent shell,
pink chunks of meat
puckering the sauce,

and this the taste: rich
and mellow, a taste
you hold in your mouth
for years—

a taste like that Virginia spring
when, hovering between lives,
we let the current carry us naked
in warm ocean waters,

and nothing else mattered—

a taste like that September leaning out
from the *S.S. Aurelia* into darkness,
green phosphorescence spinning us
through the black Atlantic—

a taste like this October afternoon,
this house a red anchor
beneath billowing leaves,
cool updrafts of wind lifting me skyward,

that long hawser stretching,
thinning itself to nothing in my wake.

FRENCH BREAD

When the north wind tears the last leaves
from the trees, and the sun of late November
peels the earth of all pretenses,
hunker down and see
what you see.
Measure everything
in ones:

one tablespoon each
of shortening, sugar, and salt
into the white ceramic bowl.
Add one cup of boiling water
followed by one of cold.

While the mixture cools to lukewarm,
drink your morning coffee, and watch
the way the light of early winter
creeps across the pine floor.

When you're ready, sprinkle one
package of dried yeast into the bowl
and wait for it to sink
to the bottom. Then slowly stir
until it dissolves. Let it stand

five minutes before adding cups
of flour—one plus one plus one—
mixing carefully with a wooden spoon
after each addition. Then continue—
one plus one—until the dough
is stiff enough to knead.

Lift it with floured hands and feel
its weight before you begin,
the heel of your hand pressing down,
fingers lifting and folding in one
continuous motion until the dough
is smooth and its surface shines
like satin. Place it in a greased bowl.

18

You will have time now
to do whatever pleases you
while the yeast expands and the sun
begins to move toward its zenith.
Maybe you'll notice
the way the bones of the earth
have surfaced, or feel the hollowness
November brings to the air

before the dough has doubled itself
beneath a checkered cloth, before
you must punch it down,
knead it once again, shape it—
one plus one plus one—into three
even loaves. Place these
on a greased baking sheet
and let them rise again

while you go in search
of whatever remains of the day.
Return within one hour
to brush the loaves
with beaten egg whites
and gently mark each one
with three diagonal slashes. Place them
in the oven at 425. Perhaps now,

as you wait precisely fifteen minutes,
you will see sun and moon
equally balanced in the late afternoon sky.
Lower the heat to 350 and continue
to bake for half an hour,
filling the house with the scent
of yeast, sugar, salt, shortening
transformed by heat
into the lightness you crave.

WILD BLUE

All six of us are eating supper
when the screen door creaks open.

No one turns to look. We know
it's just my cousin Ronnie ready to play.

Still chewing the last bite of fish stick,
I see the blue visor of his baseball cap

flashing past the openings between chairs,
hear his sneakers whacking the linoleum

as he circles the table. Finally
I'm excused, and we race outside

where the apple trees are in full bloom.
Our feet shake pink petals loose

as we clamber to the topmost branches.
Ready? I ask. *Ready!* he calls,

and we take off—
skimming the flat roof of the yellow house,

pulling on the controls and lifting up
over gardens, pine trees, graveyard—

until the wind streams through our cockpits
and open sky is all we can see.

HOPSCOTCH

Nobody told you it wasn't proper
to enter the Sheraton Athens in cut-off jeans,
but if they had, you'd've said, *Screw them!*
and done it anyway. At least
that's what you'd like to think
when your mind travels the road
to who you were then. True

or false? Who's to say
whether the sweet-tart juice
of the orange stolen from the tree
made your mouth tingle
or merely dribbled over your fingers
and dried to a sticky web
between them, whether Athens

was a city of scalding light,
scarlet poppies, honeyed baklava—
or just the sharp aftertaste
of ouzo coating the tongue,
the cry of skeletal cats
walking the narrow streets?

When you wrote home, were those postcards
meant to dazzle your mother into believing
the world you'd found held no nights
when you curled in a foreign bed
clutching the latest *Time* magazine, hungry
for a language you understood?

Or were they sent to yourself:

traveler
in another country
another time
any country
any time

but your
own?

Either way, they've been returned
in a box you're afraid to open.

HOW TO TELL YOU

This morning I found a dragonfly
in my room, thin veins of wings
nearly invisible on the white shelf
where it must have landed
sometime in the night,

bringing with it
a kaleidoscope of stars
whirling in a sky
otherwise devoid of light.

How to tell you
about perfect brown wing tips,
the arc of a dead body
beside the window?

Should I mention
the way silence overtakes the space
behind closed doors?

ON CENTRAL STREET

I remember great overarching maples and the darkness
beneath them, tight clapboards protecting our neat
New England houses, how every spring
women thinned their beds of iris, men clipped
forsythia square, and children ran wild
in the fields at dusk. I remember the long gray braids
of grandmothers wound in tight buns, and grandfathers
in heavy overcoats, thick spectacles, and the way
clocks ticked in the stale air of cluttered rooms.

On the day old Mr. Slate walked beneath his arbor,
no one heard the quiet thud of the door
behind him, the click of his car's ignition, or the rumble
of the engine. No one saw exhaust rising
in that closed space, his body slumping
against the wheel. And no one ever spoke of it,
not even the children, who watched the house darken
and the vines grow thick.

24

I SAY SUN

I say sun is a melting dream
because I don't understand.

Grown-ups hover like spiders
in the dark corners of the kitchen

and I am motionless
beneath a web of voices

speaking in whispers. I stare
at the open eye of the blackboard

that hangs on the wall
between doors, trying to choose

a direction. Grammie is dead
and my mother's absence

is an open mouth without sound.

LETTER TO MÉMÈRE

In your wedding portrait, you are perched
on the edge of flight, your body stiff
in a skirt of black taffeta, starched white blouse—
its collar holding your chin firm.
Beside you, the man who will be my grandfather
stands rigid in his best black suit,
his hair carefully parted, mustache brushed
to a fine curve. Your left hand rests
lightly on your thigh, adjusting to the weight
of the gold band, and the tips of Pépère's fingers
brush the arm of your chair. Your bodies
do not touch, but I feel how they lean
into the space between you, how your innocent
eyes widen, startled by this moment.

Years later, you find yourselves
settled on the stone wall of the farm,
your deep-set eyes looking
into the camera, your faces transformed
by the labor of nine children born and raised.
Pépère drapes his arm across your shoulder,
his hand resting on your upper arm,
denim shirt rolled above his elbows, collar open,
wrinkled overalls worn soft. Your graying hair
curls in a bun at the nape of your neck,
and your flowered dress falls in loose folds
below your knees. I look for it in your posture—
a gesture of earned love—your thickened bodies
comfortable in their closeness.

SWING

I'm thinkin' about The Big Apple,
NYC, New York, New York, Mama.
You know what I mean? Not the home
of jazz, Mama, but the place it grew up.
I'm thinkin' about Charlie the Bird Parker,
Satchmo, the Duke—any big name you want.
They were all there mixin' it up together
through those smoky nights: dancin' and jivin'
on the floors of the Savoy, men haulin' women
over their backs, women all legs, their skirts
foldin' up like flower petals around their heads—
and whiskey flowin' with the music, blacks
and whites sittin' together, rubbin' elbows,
butts movin' in their chairs to the same
beat, tappin' their feet like the keys
of a fine-tuned sax until it all fell apart
and weed turned to horse in their veins,
until they littered the bright streets of Harlem
with broken bottles, wasted bodies.
Where were you, Mama,
when all this was goin' on? Were you
sittin' by the radio in some parlor
hundreds of miles away, pressin' your ear
to the speaker, the beat throbbin' in your blood?
What were you thinkin'
when swing hit the good old USA
and you sat on a Boston bar stool
askin' for apple pie and milk, while
the whole world was explodin' around you?

AUNT EVELYN

First child of nine, she slipped away
to California, divorced, remarried in a time
when only bad women lived

with more than one man.
Her visit home an event long
awaited, much celebrated,

she and second husband Joe (those
sinners) arrived from San Diego,
a city whose very name

sounded like flamenco in our throats.
I remember her voice, deep and raspy
against my mother's mellow tones;

her dusky skin that seemed to promise
the warmth of sunlight in any season;
her flashing brown eyes watching

my mother peel thin strips of bacon
and place them in the pan. They were
two sisters reclaiming lost lives

while I inched closer, unaware
of the fat heating, expanding—
about to scorch my ivory cheeks.

WHAT SHE GAVE

I

Voices murmur in the room next door.
Muffled tears. Insistent words:
marriage, baby, regret it.
A space heater cracks and whirs,
punctuating the argument.
Who is speaking? Who
is crying?

II

The bodies in the book my mother gave me
are black and white, more
like X-rays than solid flesh.
Cross section of uterus and birth canal
like a candy-coated m&m
devoid of vagina or clitoris.
Frontal view of the ovaries,
earphones listening in on the body
through thin Fallopian tubes.
Bubbles float across a two-page spread,
egg and sperm combusting into a tiny body
curled in a comfortable sac.

III

At nineteen my mother stares out
from a black and white photo,
her eyes dancing above a curve
of white teeth, her full, luscious body
held tight in a black bathing suit,
white arms and legs carved marble
against the gray expanse of ocean.
In her innocent beauty, she is
dangerous. She is in danger.

Maybe that's why
she speaks to me now,
conversations like beads
dropped one by one
into a velvet sack.

IV
Like Thumbelina, stolen
by the frog and the mole,
you will be rescued by a beautiful bird.
You will fly on its back to safety,
your prince revealed
as petals open in the rising sun.

Silence.
Another bead drops.

Flesh too soon offered
will never be forgiven, must
live in exile. You will know
these women as yourself.

Silence.

V
I pull each bead from the sack, hold it
between thumb and forefinger,
stroke its slippery surface, listen
for what lies at the core.

I am trying to get it right:
these beads, the long silences
that beg for an ear.

KNEADING BREAD

for my mother

The morning I thought you died
was just like this.
Burnished blue sky. Sultry heat.
I stood in my kitchen
kneading bread.
My belly swelled and hardened
against the counter.
I pushed soft dough into mounds,
folded it over,
and pushed again.
You had never slept so late.
The heady aroma of yeast
filled the room,
but I saw you lying above me,
silent and immobile.
I punched the dough,
shaped it into even loaves,
pressed each in its private
pan to rise.
I knew I must climb the stairs,
open the door
and find you.
The other body inside me
rolled and shifted,
pushed against uterus walls.
I imagined every detail.
Phone calls. Arrangements to be made.
And most of all, *how to say it.*

A RECKONING

for my brother

I can't account
for the richness of my life:
gardens filled with flowers—
bee balm rising five feet tall,
phlox and primrose, peonies,
bleeding heart, cosmos—more
than I can name;
my house filled with the music of voices—
husband, children, laughter,
Mozart on piano, Goodman on clarinet,
Coltrane on sax—more sounds
than I need. And so I find myself

looking at you,
staring at what seems to be
an empty space before you.
I can't help seeing
your beard peppered white,
the gray hair curling on your collar,
and I know
I must speak, must risk
the head-on collision
with your eyes
where I see myself,
crouched in the corner of your brain,
cradling your stolen riches.

AT ST. JOHN'S

for my father

I'm searching in the shadows at the Stations
of the Cross for something to believe in.
But there is treachery here,
and Jesus hangs limp on a gold crucifix.

Ten commandments, seven sacraments:
obey and receive. Forgive me, Father,
for I have sinned.

> *They say*
> *that _you_, my father,*
> *will never be forgiven.*

Say but the Word, and you shall be healed.

> *The Word that _you_,*
> *Protestant, will never*
> *be taught.*

I finger the lavender beads of my rosary
through penance—ten Hail Marys
and five Our Fathers—and I am cleansed.

My tongue presses the host against the roof
of my mouth, where it cracks. Its starchy body
dissolves, slides to the back of my throat,
never touches my teeth. And I know salvation

is nearly mine. But am I willing
to pay the price of belief?

> *Your eternal damnation*
> *proclaimed on this cold*
> *April morning.*

SWIMMING IN FREEDOM POND

for Jeff

You tell me you dove into the universe
last night, water paralyzing your muscles,
your jaw opened by the shock
of impact. You say the risk
was worth it
to come that close
to the stars, to brush your body
against their cold light,
to lose it all
for that brief moment in the black void.

I think of midnight in Paris.
January 1970. No place to stay.
No thought
of how to get anywhere.
The stonework of the Pont Neuf
burns into the soles
of my feet, and the stars
exploding in the Seine
fill me with something foreign,
intoxicating, addictive.

But today I am your mother
and think I must tell you
diving into ponds in mid-November
shows poor judgment—
and I do.
I think I must not let you know
how I would wake this hibernating
body, swim with you,
and feel the quiver of stars.

SAY IT WAS AUTUMN

Light filters through the jeweled maple,
ripples over the rough granite rock.
My sister bellies up to it,
takes its measure,
pulls in a deep breath.
Maybe the wind blows just then,
stirring the dried leaves on the lawn.
Maybe she hears the rustle of their dead skins,
reaches for the curved top of the rock,
places the toe of her sneaker
in a crevice six inches off the ground,
hoists herself up, and balances
on her stomach until she can lift
her right leg over and straddle it.

Maybe now she begins to doubt herself
a little. But say somewhere
in the distance a crow calls. She imagines
black wings, the sensation of riding the wind,
and so gets up on her knees,
stretches her arms wide, waits
to see if balancing is possible.
Thinks it is, and so
crouches on the narrow ledge of the top—
toes curled and tense—teeters,
nearly falls, then steadies herself.

And maybe now she reconsiders,
looks down at the ground,
feels dizzy. But say the tree
shakes in the breeze again, the crow
flies across an open patch of blue
she can barely glimpse between branches.
So she rises, locks her knees,
lifts her arms until she is like Jesus
crucified in air, nailed to the emptiness
around her by the steel of her desire.

Say no one sees her in the moment
she pulls free, say her body doesn't

yield to the power of gravity, say
she rides the brilliant light
of this autumn afternoon, say she flies
on the wings of her dream.

Say she taught me how.

WHAT I WOULD DO

after reading Alice Walker's "The Snail Is My Power Animal"

what i would do is write love play breathe rise above this earth
a little let the moisture of clouds cling to the hairs on my arms
let it pebble my naked skin lap these water beads roll them on
my tongue let them slide down the chute of my throat then meet
alice share her house by the sea eat mexican food under the
melting sun talk about women and what they do and how they
feel and we'd each sit in a room of our own waiting for poems
to fall like shining copper pennies and hers would be full of snails
and coconut milk and mahogany trees and mine a fragile cup of
lavender hollow-bellied beauty and we'd gather them in our moist
palms till they're warm as skin let them fly wailing chanting
laughing in a glorious flapping of wings harmony counterpoint
syncopation riding the winds brushing the curved bodies of stars

OPENINGS

for Jeff

You were born with a hole in your heart.
Left ventricle leaking into the right,
or was it right into left? Either way,
it was a dangerous thing. I held you
in my arms, paced the length
of the hospital room again and again,
whispered a promise of protection.
The muscle knew what to do,
growing tissue to close the hole,

but tonight your heart opened again.
Turning to the audience with grace,
and more than a little fear,
you offered us your poems.
Cuffs of your baggy corduroys
pooled at your ankles, and gold threads
glittered through the scarlet
and navy stripes of your shirt.
If it weren't for your scruffy beard
you might well be eight years old again,
those same blue eyes
peering open and intent
through the round lenses of your glasses.

You speak true and simple words—
stars, black sky, teaberries on the tongue—
and give us all the magic there is
in the world you know,
your heart right up against it,
its beat melding with the rhythms you find there.
All my promises of protection are silenced,
and yes, I know it is a dangerous thing.

38

WHAT THE BODY KNOWS

I don't want to think
about that November morning,
about what pulled me back

against the forward motion
of the car, or what turned
muscle to stone, and squeezed

my heart. And I don't want to think
about how I struggled against the tears
that came, as if sprung from you

miles away in your upstairs room.
I want to remember the decision
to stop the car, and I want to believe

the call I made changed the course
of our lives. I want to be grateful.
But I'm haunted by the membrane

you pierced that day, how it might
thicken around me until I can no longer feel
the vibration of your silent call.

LEAVING AGAIN

for Alison

The car door shuts
behind you
and you walk
through darkness
toward the light.

Shoulders straight,
arch of your back firm,
ponytail bobbing,
you bounce
up the steps.

On the landing
you turn quickly,
tilt your head,
and offer
a quick flutter
of the hand,

a mysterious signal
that seems to say
the darkness between us
doesn't exist.

CHESTNUTS

I have carried them with me for weeks,
torn from the spiked green casing
that held them joined like Siamese twins,
backs pressing their weight against each other,
bodies swelling in summer rain.

On the day I left you,
I took them from the lawn beneath the tree.
I suppose I thought they might
save me on days like this,
when I can't stop looking for you here,
hoping that, like the rays of stars already dead
a thousand years, your light will flicker
on the walls of this room.

I rub my thumb across their backs,
feel how one has made itself a hollow space,
concave and ready to hold the other
in its growing, and I see faint imprints
shimmering on its surface.

Like this, I say, my body lies,
an empty mold that held you,
still radiating light.

COLLECTORS

All across America, mothers like me
are saving their children's lives:
clipping newspaper articles, photographing
first steps, first days of school, first proms.
Hoarding teddy bears, baseball caps, and whistles,
poems and stories pulled from the wilderness
of imagination and scrawled
in the large, uneven letters of childhood.

Today I watch two young girls
on the beach. Firm, round bodies
bent over the sand, they finger
slipper shells, limpets, hollow legs
of crabs. At the water's edge, their brother
snatches something white from the ground,
stands, and without hesitation
hurls it into the water.
There's three things you won't have
for your collection! he yells.

I expect an argument,
some sort of protest at least,
from the sisters, who merely turn their backs
and continue to search.
Maybe that's why I can't stop myself
from joining them. I choose
first one black stone, smooth and round
as a jelly bean, then a triangle
of frosted beach glass, two pieces of coral—

MARGIE EDWARDS FOGG

I heard when she died
they emptied her cellar
in three truckloads.
Fifteen hundred Mason jars.

I thought of how each spring
her hands had turned
the soil, planted seeds—corn
and peas, beets, cucumbers,
beans—how they had placed
tomato seedlings in rich manure.
I saw her fingers pulling free
the roots of tender sprouts—
burdock, fescue, witch grass
left to wither in the sun.

I thought of her body
bent toward earth,
gathering the harvest—
her arms straining
under the weight
of that abundance.
I saw her kitchen in the heat
of August afternoons, steam
rising from the mottled pan
to curl the hair on her brow.

How many days
of spring and summer
would it take
to guard against a famine?

CONVALESCENCE

for my father

Only the most careful cuts
with a razor could have made
this house. Quiet precision,

steel slicing cardboard,
sculpting windows, doors,
shutters. Even the straight frame

a reminder of hours waiting
for your lungs to clear,
your hands taking charge

of what they could.
I imagine your shoulders
shrouded in black,

round with coughing, and I wonder
about my black assumption
that you sat in a wooden chair,

watching the seasons
greening and dying before you.
I need to know how your hands,

thick and square as my own,
held a brush
thin enough to paint

fine cracks between clapboards,
how you lived each day in humor
watching the black wagon come and go.

HOWEVER FRAGILE

In the waning days of early October,
something in the low arc
of the sun's path across the sky
makes me fear the Earth
is wheeling off into endless darkness,
fear I'll be caught helpless
in its spin. And so I'm grateful

for three vanilla-scented candles,
for the match which sets their wicks afire,
for their light that flickers
through the cool evening hours,
turning the mind's eye translucent orange.

In this night of white stars
piercing black sky, the silver disk
of the rising moon is not enough
to bring back the brilliance
of scarlet, burnt orange, and umber
from the distant hills, not enough
to make me believe in the eternal rhythms
of darkness and light. And so, yes,

I'm grateful for these candles
bringing the golden glow of afternoon—
however fragile, however impermanent—
into the darkness of this night,
and grateful for the imagination
that believed in the power of wax
to slow the burning.

KEEPING VIGIL

I am trying to touch
what hands cannot—the breath
that heaves your chest and lifts
your shoulders. You struggle
to pull the world inside, to hold it
just a little longer.
I want to tell you to go,
I want to tell you to stay.
And so I do not speak,
but run my fingers over your swollen hand,
blue veins luminous beneath stretched skin
foreign as the flesh of a bloated fish
washed from the sea. I stroke
white bristles of hair, do not look
at the plastic tube distorting your mouth
or the gold band that cuts
your flesh. On the screens, moment
by moment, your life
is sketched in jagged green lines.
I listen to the measure of your breath
until I have the rhythm right. Only then
will I leave you, and in the semidarkness
of the waiting room, lie on a makeshift bed
trying to remember: breathe deep, breathe slow.
I fall asleep and wake again—
are you there? breathing? Yes. Yes.
Flesh from which I am made,
I am pulling you back,
I am letting you go, pulling you
back, letting you go—

A STUDY IN BLACK AND WHITE

Your tweed cap on the cotton sheets
is a study in black and white I left
hoping in some primitive way
to bring you back, although
of course I know better.

Still I let my hands
lift the cap to my face, releasing
a hint of Old Spice into the humid air,
let them turn it
so I can see
the hollow that held your head,
can stretch fingers wide
and stroke the nylon lining.

These intimate, empty spaces
startle me, the way I wake
and see your blue shirt
draped over the back of the chair
just inches from where my head
rests on the pillow, your pants
folded carefully over the arm,
and beside the bed
your footless slippers.

THE MISSION AT CAPISTRANO

Here I'm blinded by scarlet
bougainvillea staining the sun-
washed walls, and I struggle
in the relative darkness

of votive candles flickering
in that old Catholic place,
bringing back what I don't want
to remember: lenses of wire-

rimmed glasses winking in black
recesses, eyes like blue daggers,
the pursed lips of Sister Saint
Blaise here and now as she was

then and always will be,
waging war against infidels
in the one place that should,
in the aftermath of death,

bring comfort. Defiant, I light
a candle in memory of my father,
the fine blade of that old guilt
splitting me into supplicant and rebel.

WIDOWED

What am I going to do?
she pleads. I ask

what she means,
and study the outline

of my mother's lips,
which seem to be slipping

into her toothless mouth.
If I get worse, she insists,

what will I do?
She's collapsing

in on herself,
her center dissolved,

and she has
no spine, no bones

to keep her body
standing tall.

It's as if
my father took them

when he died,
took her voice, too,

which doesn't seem fair,
not fair at all.

THE WEIGHT OF BONES

She's been living in the place
where she curled
out of her body into the long stretch
of summer solstice, where light
bleached her bones
until, weightless, they floated

in shimmering heat, until they floated
so free she couldn't place
them anywhere where bones
should be, could no longer find a curl
of flesh to cushion them. Light—
they were so light that muscles couldn't stretch

to hold them. Now a stretch
of darkness floats
over her body, smothers the light.
Yes, now there is only one place
to be: in the curling
center, the meaty marrow of bones.

Here she listens to the bones
crack and snap. Unable to stretch,
they grumble in the thick curl
of joints held fast by the gristle of flesh. To float
would be so much easier, but in this place
where she longs for the light,

she will come to understand light's
treachery. Only then will she hear the bones
singing in their secret places,
only then will she stretch
into their deep rhythms and lose her desire to float.
This time her body will curl

in on itself, away from the curling
path of light
where she once floated.
This time she will follow the bones
into the mystery, the dark stretch

of winter, the place

where the curl of memory shapes bones,
sculpts a life without light. *Forget stretching,*
it says. *Forget floating. You must know this place.*

BEING THERE

I
On the night they tell me
my mother is eating less and less
each day, I have a vision:
she is resting in a fine-veined leaf,

its serrated edges turning
inward, a fragile brown cocoon
floating out of reach
on a curve of invisible energy.

II
My mother's mouth is tight
with unspeakable pain,
and her white hair fans out
like startled feathers
around her pale face.

She is wrapped in a white
blanket from neck to feet,
and cold April rain
pummels the black umbrella
above her head. A driver
wheels her to the van

where she is miraculously lifted.
Our eyes meet in the moment
before she is swallowed up.

III
In the van my mother closes
her eyes and moans
as we hit pothole after pothole,
and her wheelchair bounces and dips,
straining against the straps
meant to hold her in place.

IV
White on the nose and forehead,
shallow irregular breathing,
mottled skin, cold hands and feet—

52

these are the signs to look for,
they tell me, as I stand watch.
No one can say when

it will happen. My mother's eyes
move beneath closed lids.
I take her hand,

apply gentle pressure,
and begin to sing softly,
Amazing grace, how sweet

the sound . . . Her hand flutters,
soft as birdsong against my skin,
and a smile flickers across her face.

V
It's midnight and I'm afraid
to tell anyone the sign
that makes me know:

white foam is rising
into her mouth,
filling it, beginning

to spill out at the corners.
I wipe it away, knowing
she wouldn't want us to see.

VI
12:15 a.m.
Impossible stillness
in the wake
of her leaving.

ALWAYS THIS FALLING

My mother, who loved all objects with a history,
would've been drawn by the word ANTIQUES
in block letters on the side of a red barn.

She would've been willing to enter the darkness
and search the clutter on counters and shelves,
to wait for a shaft of autumn sunlight

to transform cut glass to gold, inviting her
to become the caretaker of unspoken stories.
Now she's left this work for me. I hold a cruet

in the white light of winter, try to imagine
a man polishing its flashing surface, sliding
his thumbnail in the deep crystal grooves,

satisfied by the way he's cut five suns
rising above feathered stalks of wheat,
try to picture the first moment

his fingers touched the tools
that one day would give solid shape
to his imaginings. I want it to be endless,

this dreaming backward into history
where one thing leads to another and another,
and there is always this falling

into a fine spun web of light, but already
the sun has shifted, leaving this vessel
transparent and voiceless in the silent room.

MEMORIAL DAY

This morning I work the black soil,
bone-white stems of last year's flowers
turning in my hands—all that remains
of your last planting
before the stones of your ancestors.
I place seedlings in that cradle of darkness,

then break new ground
for red geraniums
whose roots will probe the earth
where you now lie.
I lift and shake the sod
until a pile of dirt collects,
then spread its warmth
beneath the leaves. Now

I walk the cemetery roads
in search of water, hear
a bird I cannot name
calling from the maples. His song
keeps time with my steps
from spigot to grave and back,
again and again, cold water spilling out
over the edge of the pan.

"FOR SALE: BY ORDER OF THE REMAINING HEIRS"

after Theodore Roethke

Finally, there is no one left
to nail the window in place.
Moonlight shivers
across the snow, and shadows
of the horse chestnut
creep toward the house.

The window is free
to slide from its frame
and fall with a hollow sound.
Plaster walls crack and crumble,
sifting down to settle
over the echo of footsteps.

Now wind drums soft against the clapboards,
ghostly feet stamp the dust,
and images grow in the mottled mirror—
selves behind selves,
looking for words to flower
like red peonies in sweet summer flesh.

Outside, lavender loosestrife
runs amok in the yard,
petals fall from silent stems,
shaking free the dream-seed—

AT THE CENTER

I
This will be the last day of your life.
You know this
because you woke to a flash of darkness,
a moment of absolute silence.

The lilac outside your window
casts a sharp shadow on the wall.
A white-throated sparrow sings,
Oh Sam Peabody, Peabody, Peabody,
and you long for one last call
of the loon across the lake.

The cat curls on your legs,
vibrations of his contented body
settling into your shins, calves, belly.
Above your head, footsteps
cross the bedroom floor.

II
The smell of percolating coffee
fills the air. You fold fresh raspberries
into the sweet batter of waffles. Soon
the delicate flavor of maple
mixes with the tang of fruit
on your tongue. You reach
across the table, gently stroke
the back of your husband's hand.

You feel a sudden collapse of sound,
your eardrums being sucked into your brain.
The world moves in slow motion,
a mouth forms words you can't hear,
the rhythm of leaves blowing in the wind
becomes a visual song. This is the first step
in a solitary journey.

III
Milkweed spices the humid air, sunlight
gilds the skeleton of the old barn
on the hill. Everything that moves
floats. Suspended in the absence
of sound, a door moves but never closes,
cars glide without stopping. You wait
for an end that never arrives.

When bee balm sends long shadows
across the lawn, you return to the house.
Now is the time for tart, dry wine, the chill
of the goblet against your fingers.
You watch the prism in your window
turn in the breeze. Red, magenta, green,
and gold flash from its surface, ripple
over the pine floor. You feel the coldness
of the wine in your mouth and throat,
its sudden warmth
when it reaches your stomach,
moves through every extremity.
You taste nothing.

IV
As the sun slips beneath the horizon,
you go to the edge of the field,
only half believing you might be filled
with the scent of new-mown hay. By now
you know this is a day for emptying.
The sky confirms this. Gone
from rose to gray, it deepens—charcoal, ebony.